How To Live a Soft Life:

Using The Power of Feminine Energy

Written by Reemus

COPYRIGHT

This is the third part of the Femininity Series

Volume 1: Healing the Feminine Energy & The Wounds of Your Inner Child

Volume 2: Nurturing Your Feminine Energy & The Rise of Divine Femininity

Volume 3: How To Live A Soft Life: Using The Power Of Feminine Energy

Note: It is highly recommended to read the first volume before reading this book. The concepts mentioned in this book are a continuation of the first volume of the series.

TABLE OF CONTENTS

INTRO

"A soft life is one of peace, comfort and intentional happiness. It does not require struggle or stress. It consists of reciprocity, support, flow and self-care.

It's the embracing of an experience that includes ease and relaxation. It's knowing that you are worthy as you are, yet with the inspiration to be your highest self.

A soft life is the ultimate act of self-love in a world that wants you to remain hard."

- Reemus

The Meaning of a Soft Life

The aim of this book is to support you in attaining an emotional state that makes life worth living. Some would call this "the pursuit of happiness". But what makes this particular pursuit different is that we are going to take the spiritual path, do deep internal work, and utilise the power of feminine energy to achieve this.

Many people try to find contentment by acquiring things like cars, money or jewellery. You have others that try to find it through plastic surgery, food or endless vacations to escape their everyday life. Then you also have some people who use partners or sex to find contentment.

There's no doubt that these things do bring pleasure on some level. But it's pleasure that lacks true depth. Real everlasting pleasure is available through creating a reality that fosters peace, ease and safety. And it's important you know that for it to be sustainable, this reality must first be cultivated within you.

When your internal state is not one of harmony, no change on the outside will be good enough to satisfy you long term. But when you pour positivity, love and empowerment into yourself, satisfaction suddenly becomes readily available. Then, your outer world begins to mirror the internal one.

Much peace is found when we heal, nurture and embody the energetic state that our bodies are designed to express. As we covered in the first book of this series: "*Healing the Feminine Energy: & The Wounds of Your Inner Child*", there are two tools that you have available to use in order to interact with the world: the physical body and the spiritual body.

The physical body is what we use to interact with the physical 3D world through our senses. The spiritual body houses our energy. And if we want to have true fulfilment, then both the physical and spiritual body must align and be in a balanced state.

In the case of women, this means being connected to feminine energy. For men, it is generally the opposite. The 'core' energy that a man's spiritual body seeks to express is masculine energy.

Regardless of what gender you are, you will naturally express both energies. However, you'll notice that you feel fulfilled when the dominating energy that you express is the one that matches your physical body.

The focus of this particular book is to guide you to tap into feminine energy in such a way that you release stress, tension and anxiety by simply embracing softness. Softness is usually seen as a weakness, but we're going to discover how and why this is not true.

There are major strengths in softness. When you take pride in this, you are empowered with confidence, authenticity and magnetism. You'll begin to cultivate a successful life that doesn't have to feel difficult and exhausting.

Working on your feminine energy is a journey that gets easier as you go further along the path. But it's important to commit to stay on it, otherwise you won't get the benefits that await on the other side.

Though the desire to have a "soft life" is becoming trendy, it's important to know that it's more than a trend; it's a way of living. In this book, the aim is to heal the connection between your spiritual and physical body so that you live a life that is aligned with your feminine powers.

Your Mind Creates Your Reality

Aligning the spiritual and physical bodies brings fulfilment. However, there is another important part to this that plays a major role: it is the mind (which could be considered as the *'mental body'*).

The mind is a machine that filters the information that comes through your senses. It is like an intermediary between the physical and spiritual body. It's responsible for the way that you view things. The thoughts, beliefs and statements that exist in your mind play a major role in influencing how you feel.

Have you ever listened to a song that was so catchy that, even when you stopped listening to it, the lyrics endlessly played in your mind? This shows your mind's ability to pick up certain words and play them on repeat.

The same thing happens to the thoughts and beliefs that you allow to exist in your mind.

Many of those thoughts are placed there by outside sources such as parents, friends, the education system and (mass and social) media 'teaching' us what to think.

These external influences are what shape our internal reality. Like the catchy song that plays in your mind, the beliefs that we're given play automatically too. They shape how we think and feel about ourselves. How we feel about ourselves is then what continues to manifest through our actions.

The problem is that the thoughts we often hold onto do not serve us well. Let's take this example: most women (and men) grow up believing that the expression of femininity is a weakness. These negative thoughts play in the minds of women and have a heavy effect on how they move through the world.

Most women end up abandoning their feminine energy and express themselves in a masculine way. They don't receive affirmations of the fact that femininity is a woman's greatest power.

They aren't told that softness is a beautiful thing and something that every woman deserves to have in her life. Through words, actions or life situations, women are dissuaded from being soft.

Much of the world seems to be an endless affirmation of the very opposite: that a woman needs to be 'hard' to survive in this world. Unfortunately, this ends up creating a lack of satisfaction because it's in a woman's primal nature to be the expression of femininity.

She soon finds out that life is not that fun when she has to be hard all of the time. It becomes tiring always being in 'survival' mode. It becomes frustrating constantly living with your masculine shield up. It becomes exhausting forever needing to carry this weight.

There will come a time when she wants to rid herself of the burden that comes from having a masculine mindset so that she can experience the bliss that feminine embodiment provides.

The Power of Affirmations

Though it can be difficult to 'let go' of the mindset which prevents you from embracing softness, it certainly isn't impossible. Your mind needs to begin prioritising the qualities of the Feminine. The key is to change the 'catchy song' that is playing over and over again in your subconscious mind. Through changing how you speak to your inner child, you are going to heal your entire reality.

The stories that you keep telling yourself about who you are determine how you interact with the world. This is powerful because you have the power to change your story, and in turn, alter your inner and outer worlds. Realise that everything you see is a manifestation of your mind. And when you learn how to live in-tune with your thoughts, you begin to change your reality.

You are truly empowered when you realise this because you learn that you are the designer of your world. You'll only befriend those who align with your mind, enter environments that allow you to feel safe and do things that support your softness. You'll simply let go of the things that aren't for you because you know that it doesn't belong in your reality.

Throughout the chapters in this book, be prepared to find sections of "affirmations" that you can repeat. Knowledge is great, but what is the purpose of it if it doesn't have a positive impact on your life? So be sure to do the guided affirmations so that you get the most out of this book.

Make a commitment that over the next month (*one to three months is ideal*) you'll put in the effort to change how you speak to yourself and redesign the thoughts in your mind. When you repeat the affirmations, place your hand on your heart and imagine that you are pouring new beliefs into yourself.

Without a shadow of a doubt, the way you feel about yourself will change. Each day, repeat one section of affirmations at least five times. And do it at least three times a day (morning, afternoon and night). Do it with intention. Your inner child is there and deserves to hear powerful expressions of self-love.

Keep in mind that affirmations are statements that reaffirm who you are, *not* what you want to be. You are already who you want to be. It's just about bringing that expression into the light. So affirmations are done in the present tense ("I am…"), rather than the future tense (I will be…").

Starve the negative self-talk you've been allowing to exist in your mind. Whenever you catch yourself talking about yourself in a negative way, stop it and immediately tell yourself 3-6 statements of a positive nature. Over time, you'll replace the negativity with positive affirmations.

If you take anything from this book let it be this: the way you speak to yourself is of utmost importance. You are an expression of royalty; a divinely designed embodiment of beauty and you deserve to live in a world that grants you fulfilment. The flowers of these seeds start with the beliefs that you plant inside of yourself.

THE STRENGTH IN SOFTNESS

Traits of The Empowered Soft Woman

- She establishes firm boundaries
- Her compassionate presence is soothing
- She has enthusiasm about life and shares it with those around her
- She is proud of having a heart full of affection or kindness
- She loves love
- She prioritises peace, patience and positivity
- Lives with good intentions for herself and others
- Holds faithfulness in her heart and trusts divine guidance
- She takes pride in her pleasure
- She feels deserving of serenity and bliss
- She doesn't allow the negativity of others to poison the positivity in her heart

What it Means to be "Soft"

The world can feel unfathomably difficult at times. Most of us have experienced situations that have required us to harden up in order to survive. As the saying goes *"tough times don't last, tough people do"*. Unfortunately, what *can* last is the effect that those tough times have had on you.

Even when the situation has passed and we've made it through to the other side, our spirit remains hardened as it retains the traumatic impact linked to the experience. As we touched on in the first volume of the *'Femininity Series'* in "*Healing the Feminine Energy: & the Wounds of Your Inner Child*", there are so many different circumstances that call upon the masculine shield to come out.

There are different reasons why the inner masculine shield will come out to protect you. Perhaps it was a breakup, or maybe it was a rough childhood, or even being abandoned by a parent who told you they'd never leave. Whatever it is, we've all been through some form of trauma.

Tending to your inner child is the key to putting you on the path of softening up. However, this only heals the spiritual body. If you don't also align your daily thoughts, lifestyle and your environment in accordance with softness, then you won't be able to maintain a soft state for a prolonged time.

Everyone deserves to live a life that is aligned with authenticity, flow and ease. But many people have been discouraged from taking the route of a soft life to do so. They think that softness is weakness. But this is not true. Softness doesn't equal weakness. It can be one of your greatest strengths.

Think about anything that is soft. It could be play-dough or candy floss. It could even be a pillow. Th quality of being soft is the reason why it can't be broken. It's the hard things that can be broken. Go ahead and try to punch your pillow. It will simply absorb the force and breath right back into shape. This is why the feminine spirit is so magnificent.

Softness allows you to mould to the challenges that life presents. It's what truly makes you unstoppable. No matter how hard life gets, your internal softness provides a space for life to be breathed right back into you. And this is why you should be endlessly proud of your feminine qualities.

Softness is Safe

Expressing softness in an empowered way doesn't mean you have to give up your individual style or who you are. In fact, it's quite the opposite. Softness grants you the luxury of giving up the things that *stop* you from being who you truly are. It strips away the remnants of past traumas and difficulties. It's about letting go rather than holding on. You can release your attachment to stress so that you are left with inner peace.

If you want to start living a "soft life", you have to tell yourself that you deserve the right to live in such a way that doesn't force you to embrace hardness.

After deciding that you are worthy of a "soft life", it's now time to be the embodiment of this intention. It's time to live a life that represents this. Set the intention to rebrand as a new version of yourself.

You are no longer the woman who is used to predominately relying on her masculine energy. That is no longer you, and you're going to let it all go. You are now the beautiful feminine woman who lives a gentle life of inspiration and vibrancy. Don't allow your mind to come up with reasons why this isn't true. Feed yourself with the affirmations that tell you that this is who you are and this has always been who you are destined to be.

You are no longer the woman who has to choose combativeness, conflict or withdrawal as your primary go-to. That's a life based on fear and being in survival mode. You no longer allow your triggers or emotions to rule you. You royally rule over them. You are now open to receiving the highest version of you.

The modern day world can feel harsh on women. So the hard masculine shield often needs to come out for protection. But being addicted to that shield and using it even when circumstances don't call for it can be exhausting and unfulfilling. This is particularly true when you consider that most times, it's not as necessary as we *think* it is.

Being able to embrace the power of softness gifts you a choice. You can transition between softness and hardness according to when it's required rather than out of fear. This allows you to connect to your heart and your body, rather than always living in the head and the mind.

Many times, we want the world to make us feel safe. But if this is the mindset you have, I can warn you that you'll be waiting a very long time unfortunately.

It's more empowering to realise that you are the most influential part of your life. This should make you excited, because it means that life is exactly what *you* choose to make it.

A woman who knows that she deserves the bliss of tenderness in her heart is soft with *herself* first. We enter into relationships and friendships demanding that we are loved. And we get offended when we feel that we aren't getting the love we deserve. But a woman who's totally in love with herself usually doesn't have these problems. Her self-love is reflected in those she allows to be around her.

It sounds simple, but have you been loving yourself to the highest degree? When you woke up this morning, did you tell yourself how much you love yourself? Do you remember to shower yourself with positive self-talk that transcends any love that others could ever give you?

Make it a goal to talk to yourself with love and kindness. When you make a mistake, don't talk down to yourself. You are the most important being in your reality. So treat yourself like it. Instead of saying "I'm so stupid, what's wrong with me?", say: "Mistakes happen and we'll do even better next time!"

It sounds like a minor thing but I assure you that it's not. Cut out *all* negative self-talk. There's no situation that is significant enough to justify being harsh to yourself. It doesn't matter what the circumstance is.

Be kinder to yourself. Remember that living a life that's aligned with love is the minimum standard for someone as great as you.

Affirmations - Connect to Femininity:

"I connect to my feminine energy and I am a radiant expression of beauty."

"I love being feminine. It brings me joy."

"It feels so good to be a woman."

"I'm a beautiful manifestation of softness and femininity."

"My feminine energy is strong and it touches everything around me."

"I feel magnificently feminine and it feels amazing."

"My feminine energy is increasing each and every day."

"I deserve to feel soft and it is safe to be soft in my reality."

"Femininity is not a weakness. It is my greatest power."

"Feminine energy flows through every fibre of my being."

Softening Yourself

Living a "soft life" is about more than just nights out at a restaurant or being taken care of in a relationship by a loving partner. Those things are great but we also want to design a life capable of connecting us to softness in *every* area possible.

So a "soft life" in its entirety includes:

- Softening your mind (releasing anxiety, worries and doubts)

- Softening your heart (expressing beauty, peace and ease)

- Softening your body (moving with sensuality and presence)

- Softening your expression (speaking with authenticity, consideration and confidence)

If you only allow yourself to be 'soft' in one area, is it really a soft life? All of these aspects are linked to each other. And improving in each area is how you can create a reality that is soft internally and externally.

The longer you stay committed to the journey, the more you'll soften up in ways you never thought possible. You'll end up letting go of the attachments you have to your triggers. You'll become more open, which is the key you need to magnetise good fortune into your life.

One powerful exercise you can do is to sit down and think back to a time in your life when you truly felt soft, safe and seen. Play the scenario back in your mind and tap into the power of visualisation. How good did it feel? What were the things that made it possible? What type of environment were you in and who was in it? How were you speaking and interacting with yourself?

Set this feeling as the standard and expectation for your life. This feeling shouldn't feel like a state that is out of reach. It's available to you now. All you have to do is reach out and connect with it.

Affirmations - The Commitment to Soften:

"I release the hardness and welcome the softness within me."

"I'm in my soft girl era/ I'm in my soft era."

"I'm a beautiful expression of divine work."

"My heart is a sanctuary of safety for my spirit."

"My essence magnetises love, support and kindness from the world."

"I soften my grip on control. I allow life to unfold."

"My comfort is my priority and I invite the experience of peace and tranquillity into my life."

"I choose to let go of hardness. I let go of the need to be guarded. I deserve a life full of ease and flow."

"I prioritise the embodiment of femininity and I live in an environment that supports my softness."

RELEASE STRESS AND STRUGGLE

"Do not let the world make you hard. Stay soft and invite the world to follow suit." **– Reemus**

Prioritise ease

Society encourages us to believe that struggle is necessary to feel valuable. Without a doubt, hard work and consistency is obviously required to enact successful change in our lives. However, this doesn't mean we *aren't* valuable if we don't live a life of struggle.

Unfortunately, many women take pride in their ability to sustain themselves through long periods of stress. They see it as a badge of honour in quite the same way that a soldier sees battle scars. They have married their minds to the idea of struggling, whether they are consciously aware of it or not.

If you are okay with living a life of struggle in order to get what you want, then that's fine. There's no right or wrong way. But this is not the way to go if you'd like to embrace your feminine energy. When you are in your masculine, you are in go-mode, forever 'doing' and pushing out into the world. Being feminine is about embracing relaxation.

Be proud of the struggles that you have overcome. But don't attach your sense of self-worth to the idea that a life of struggle is necessary. Know that you don't have to live a life of stress to feel worthy.

You are valuable and successful as you are, as long as you remain in a state of inspiration and constant self-development. See the cultivation of your spirit as your greatest strength because this is what will bring you the most fulfilment.

Doesn't life feel more satisfying when we have less to worry about? We are only required to be as hard as our environment needs us to be.

It's natural that some circumstances will require you to call upon typically masculine traits. However you are only required to be hard for those hard times. Being in your feminine energy should be the priority at all other times.

So don't get married to the idea of labour. Instead, make an intention for peace and ease instead. I invite you to no longer view hardness as a state that's more admirable than softness. Do you accept this invitation?

Affirmations - Invite Ease:

"I am worthy of peace and a life full of ease."

"I am fully deserving of a life that is free from tension and stress."

"I don't chase, I attract."

"I attract success with my feminine energy."

"I release the need to struggle."

"I am at peace with all that is."

"I embrace my feminine essence of receptivity, intuition, and nurturing."

"I am a source of value so I attract value."

"I don't chase goals. I create the conditions that magnetise the value that I want."

"I am at peace with myself."

Invite Comfort

One of the best ways to live a life that's soft is to simply ask: *"does this action or lifestyle I'm engaging in help, heal or soothe my heart? Or does it hurt, tire or stress my heart?"*. Ask yourself if what you're doing adds difficulty to your life. This puts you on the path to approaching life with gentleness.

'Less' is definitely 'more' when it relates to feminine embodiment. This requires a mindset shift from what the norm in society is. An empowered feminine woman doesn't see any reason to make things any more energetically taxing than they need to be.

When we think about the meaning of the word "gentle", consider the definition as being *"the lightness with which a situation is being approached."* And this is the energy that a feminine woman attracts, as she is the embodiment of gentleness herself.

People see her connection to softness and approach her with great consideration. They are invested in contributing towards a reality that serves her emotional contentment.

Women who project hyper independence or toughness don't magnetise the help of others. For example, a woman who constantly tells the world she "doesn't need anyone" will attract treatment that mirrors this statement.

Others will watch you struggle or exert yourself without asking if you need support because they think that you can handle it all by yourself. And you cannot really blame them since this is how you taught them to interact with you. However, people should see you and *want* to come to provide assistance or value. It doesn't mean that you *can't* carry out tasks by yourself. But the question is: why would you *want* to if you don't *have* to? This doesn't make you weak or less than. It makes you smart, as you can utilise the resources around you to your advantage. This is a truly powerful position to be in.

The queen of the castle doesn't indulge in the hard labour of the kingdom. She has people excited and willing to assist her. And they feel that it's an honour to do so. They want to see her relax in her royal state. So remember, less is more. It's okay to do things in moderation. Set the conscious intention to allow yourself to be taken care of when life offers you help.

Let's imagine there are two ladies. The first lady is a feminine woman who is confident and self-assured, whilst being inviting and magnetic in her energy. She knows that she doesn't want to do everything herself so she accepts assistance where it's offered and graciously thanks those who make her life easier.

On the other hand, the second lady leads with her masculine shield. She may be loved by others but she is seen as completely self-sufficient. When offered help, she quickly dismisses the offer, stating that she is fine to do it herself. She likes the idea of being fiercely independent as it makes her feel better about herself.

Who do you think is more likely to attract assistance? People would be more likely to rush to the aid, protection and service of the first lady. They may know that she can do everything herself, but they don't feel the desire to allow her to do so. The second lady doesn't invite the assistance of others as she has let other people know that she doesn't want help. So they don't give it to her.

Which lady would you rather be: the one who attracts acts of service or the one left to do it all by herself? The first option invites softness.

This same standard must be adopted into daily living. Begin to become aware of what it feels like to be at peace. Fall in love with the comfort that comes when you feel relaxed. Use this as the compass that influences your actions.

Modify the decisions you make, the environments you are in and the people around you, according to what maintains that feeling of peace. This can be applied to all areas of life, including work, social interactions and more.

Whenever you feel yourself on the verge of leaving that baseline of comfort, ask yourself: *is there an easier way to do this?* You'll find that this motivates you to drop all the habits that don't contribute towards your fulfilment.

You'll stop engaging in conversations that threaten to move you out of a peaceful state. You'll stop prioritising being a hard worker as opposed to being a smart worker.

You'll begin to be more flexible with your plans so that you can do what makes you feel good rather than sticking to routines that don't allow you to align with your present state of emotions.

When you set comfort as the baseline standard for your life and decide you don't want to leave that feeling when it's unnecessary, your entire approach to life will drastically change.

The Power of Release

One of the most pleasing experiences that feminine embodiment provides is the pleasure of releasing. Embracing femininity calls you to release and surrender all that doesn't serve you and your highest good. The more you can let go and release, the more ease you feel in your heart.

There is only so much that we can store before it begins to feel like an overwhelming burden. We could be storing trauma, pain, heavy responsibilities, resentment and the list goes on. It all depends on your specific experiences. Regardless, you must practise the art of letting go and feeling internal surrender.

It must become a habit to feel yourself internally 'let go' whenever you feel tension. This could look like stopping to take a deep breath to literally relax your shoulders and any areas where tension has been stored.

The physical placement of the tension is the area you want to focus on. Next, energetically let go by shifting your awareness into the present moment and releasing any burdens.

Physically relaxing is one aspect, but mentally letting go of things will take a little bit more work. It will require the understanding that you need to stop holding onto mental attachments that are weighing you down. This requires the acceptance that you are here to commit to certain things but other burdens and responsibilities are simply not yours to carry. You must grant yourself the permission to release the responsibilities that don't serve you and that are not yours in the first place.

Depending on where you currently are, this may be difficult. You may be the woman who has signed up to be responsible for the wellbeing of others. For example, let's say that you have given people around you the permission to depend on you for help even when it inconveniences you.

These people may feel comfortable interrupting your periods of self-care to ask for your advice or to get you to carry out favours for them. Or it could be that your work colleagues expect you to do tasks that help them out but it takes away time that you need for your own work. Alternatively, your friends may emotionally dump their latest complaints on you even when you're going through your own difficulties.

Whatever the case may be for your specific situation, it's important to assess how *you* feel about taking on the responsibilities of other people's issues. Be honest and ask yourself if you have the capacity to serve others and then commit to not overextending yourself past your limit.

Release the belief that you are responsible for the wellbeing of others. Release the idea that you are responsible for the happiness or satisfaction of others. Aside from those who you truly are responsible for, such as your immediate family or those you care for (including children or elderly relatives), it's not your responsibility.

Doing this will release the spiritual and mental load that you have been carrying for so long. Let your body tell you how far you are able and willing to serve, and go no further than that. If it requires you politely, but firmly, drawing boundaries with people to let them know that you don't have the capacity to help, then let this be the outcome.

If this causes strife amongst some people who feel entitled to your energy, then allow this to be the case. Release any feeling of guilt that you may have about adopting this mindset, with the understanding that you are only here to serve others as far as you have a healthy capacity to do so.

Let go of the fear of what may happen if you disappoint others who have become comfortable resting their burdens upon you. No matter what happens, there is safety within yourself as long as you trust yourself. If you lose friends as a result of practising this kind of spiritual self-care, then those people don't align with the empowered feminine woman you are becoming.

What good is it to serve the world if you are the one on the losing end? This mindset is how to avoid being taken advantage of or depleting yourself. Many women who are empathetic or nurturing allow themselves to overextend, naïvely forgetting that people will use you if you tolerate it.

Allowing this to happen is certainly not the empowered expression of softness. You must be willing to fiercely protect your energy. You do that by releasing the things that don't serve you and making no apology for it.

Affirmations - Commit to Release:

"I inhale relaxation. I breathe out all the tension."

"I am grounded in the present."

"I let my heart lead the way. My path unfolds gently."

"The burdens of others are not mine to carry. I'm only here to serve as far as what makes me comfortable."

"I release the idea that I am a burden. I make space for others to help me."

"I release the need to control. I trust in the flow of life."

"I release judgement and allow myself to radiate freely. I release myself from the hold of other people's opinions."

"My opinion is the only one which holds dominion in my reality."

"I release the need to know. I welcome change and growth. I am adaptable."

"I surrender outcomes. I am divinely directed and spirituality protected."

Be Gentle with the World

Set the intention of being gentle with the world. Think about how you tend to plants, pets and the people you love. You do it with compassion. Be a beautiful reservoir of love and kindness to others. Though other people will benefit from this mindset, the main beneficiary is you. This is because to give love, you first must be in possession of it yourself.

Likewise, when you have negative vibes within, you suffer from holding it inside of you. It's a major act of self-care to live with positivity. When you are filled with the spirit of love on a daily basis, it's invigorating. It's healing to your mind and heart.

There are certain changes that you can make to your mindset so that you interact with the world holding love in your heart:

- **Stop judging others.** You can still be encouraging towards them even if you

need to point out places for
improvement.

- **Don't be demanding,** or commanding,
when asking other people to do things.
Make requests in a way that's inviting
and inspiring.

- **Practice being empathetic** and
understanding rather than being
argumentative and defensive.

- **Seek to understand** people and see
things from their point of view.

- **Seek the consent of others** when you
are taking action that may directly affect
them. Check in and see that whatever
experience you're sharing with them is
okay with them.

One of the most powerful things you can do is
to see the point of view that other people are
coming from. Knowing the pain points of those
around you allows you to avoid situations of
conflict. However, don't confuse this with
pandering or people-pleasing. This is not what
we are talking about. It's simply that you are

doing the actions that help to maintain a positive environment around you.

When you are open to other perspectives, you naturally stop judging others. This may sound surprising but when you stop judging others, you become less conscious of the judgement that other people could have towards you. It's almost like you forget that judgement is even a thing, so you are more emboldened and free to be your authentic self.

Many people are held back by what others think of them. Fear of judgement stops people in so many different areas of life. But when you are soft with your mind, this will no longer be something that holds you back.

Anxiety comes from holding onto tension in the mind. And worries arrive when you're holding onto thoughts and visualisations that induce negative feelings. Release your attachment to the thoughts that hold you back. There are no worries inside your body about the past or the future, so in your body is where your awareness should reside. All worries are spawned in your mind. It's in the body where you can be present with the flow of the moment, giving you the ability to be your most authentic self and cater to your needs.

Think about a time when you went out with your friends to the nightclub, or perhaps when you went sightseeing on vacation, and you were totally free from the worries of the mind. The reason you weren't worried was because you were living in your body. You were fully present. Remember that this feeling of freedom is available to you at *any time*.

Boundaries & Dealing with Conflict

It's difficult to stay soft if the world you are in forces you to be hard. So refrain from being in situations or around people that don't make you feel safe, seen and heard. Why put yourself in situations that don't support you being who you want to be?

As nice as it sounds to expect the world to be soft with you *all* of the time, this isn't exactly realistic. So it's a necessity to be able to know how to deal with conflict so that you can minimise the intensity of the situation. This will counterintuitively make you more confident about expressing softness because you know that you're able to handle yourself when certain situations arise.

Understand that there are people out there who are quick to resort to combativeness. Although they may seem tough, the truth is that they are usually acting out of fear. Think of road rage for example. When people get mad at other drivers because of a mistake that was made on the road, what they are *really* saying is *"I'm terrified because I was fearful for my life!"*. Their outrage came from fear. So don't take it personally.

Learn to respond to conflict in a firm but detached manner. Firmness is important because it dissuades people from disrespecting or walking all over you. Disrespect is to never be tolerated and boundaries are the only way to protect yourself. See yourself as too worthy to be mistreated. But try not to become emotionally attached to the situation enough for it to leave a stain on your emotional state.

This is the power of being detached because your emotional state is not at the mercy of someone or something else. Other people should not have the power to control how you feel with such ease. Just because they decided to be negative, does this mean that you should be too?

Do not allow their negativity to become a part of you or to have a hold over you. Letting this happen means you are giving your power away. As your self-love increases, this will begin to become less of a struggle. It's an act of self-love to uphold a positive emotional state. When you love yourself, you see yourself as worthy enough for this type of experience.

Many times, having a soft approach to communication will get people to release their negativity, as long as you remain confident and firm. Think "how can I collaborate with this person or situation so that we can both get what we want" rather than thinking "how can I fight against them so I can get what I want". When you show them that you're on their team and that you're here to help rather than hurt, it lowers their guard.

Remember, the point of this is not to appease or allow yourself to be taken advantage of. The point is to invite security into your interactions so that you don't let tension seep into your day.

There are some people who are so settled in their toxicity that no amount of encouragement is going to change it. They may be committed to being combative. In these cases, you have no choice but to remove yourself from the situation. This preserves the softness of your reality.

Let Go of the Ego

The 'ego' is your personal projection of the type of persona that you are attached to. The ego is formed from the beliefs you have about the world and your place in it. It's the projection of what you believe to be the right or wrong way of life. It's a sense of personal identity that motivates you to play a certain role. In this culture, many people live in a way that is led by their ego.

The problem is that you are not the ego. You are not a character. You are not a 'role' that's attached to a certain way of being. You are a spirit who is experiencing the world around you through your mind and body, with the use of the senses you have been gifted.

The spiritual side of you is a little different to the ego. When you let your spirit lead with love and light, you aren't triggered into fight-mode.

You don't experience being 'offended'. You let go of the feeling that you have to defend your ego, your persona and your set of beliefs.

For example, let's say you are in a conversation with another person who has a different political opinion to you. Your ego will want you to tell them that they are wrong. Now your body triggers stress signals at the mere thought of their difference of opinion.

Your body literally feels chemically encouraged to get you to impose your beliefs on the other person. This is why you'll often see people fighting and abusing each other over their conflicting opinions. It's quite insane when you think about it.

A more positive alternative would be for them to encourage each other's personal expression, even if it's different from their own beliefs. Instead of hating each other for a different point of view, they could inquisitively ask why they believe what they believe and if they could learn anything from it.

Whenever you feel yourself reacting to someone in an attempt to validate your ego, stop and release. Be aware that you're being triggered and that you're trying to protect yourself. Know that it's okay. You are safe and you don't need to call upon the masculine guard to harden you up. You can stay soft, detaching yourself from the negativity that they're trying to incite.

When you put your ego in the backseat, you realise that many things that trigger you only have the power to do so because *you* give them power. True empowerment comes when your sense of security is not interrupted by the opinion of others or the seeking of validation and acceptance. You can choose to simply let go and feel the light that is in your heart.

Most people are quick to enter attack and defence mode. As soon as they hear something they disagree with or see something they don't like, the emotional distress they experience feels intense. Their level of contentment is literally dictated by other people's actions.

This is why a soft mindset is a strength. Softness offers security that the state of hardness does not offer.

Softness allows you to let go of the ego. It encourages you to let the love and light that resides within remain unaffected by the conflict that others try to bring.

You Don't Need to Prove Yourself

You have to let go of all notions that you need to prove yourself to anyone. The ego seeks approval from others. But when you bathe your spirit in the pool of self-love, no approval from anyone else is needed. You immediately stop exerting energy seeking the acceptance of others.

This mindset is incredibly empowering. It prevents you from trying to prove yourself as 'right' or protect yourself from being 'wrong'. It stops you from using sex or love to please partners in an attempt to fill voids in your self-esteem. It allows you to accept that the way you are is enough, and if that is not good enough for others, you remain unbothered.

It's harder to be triggered when you stay in the spirit of softness because you're living in the purity of the heart where there is no ego. You don't seek to be right. You don't seek to be anyone's idea of perfection. You don't beat yourself up for making mistakes. You don't care what anyone thinks of you.

You don't go through life thinking you need to defend yourself or attack others, because you are at peace with yourself. It's an illusion of the mind to think that everything needs to be taken to heart. When you're triggered, that is not you. It's the pain. It's the fear.

You need to simply meet all fear and pain with love and light. There is strength in rising above the challenges that usually trigger you. Think of yourself as a queen who is too big to be bothered by the petty situations being brought to you.

The value of your heart is so high that not everyone or everything should have direct access to it. So maintain the bliss of your mind by not being easily triggered by the things or people around you.

Bring that same sense of calmness into your conversations. Don't be quick to get argumentative when you disagree with someone. And don't get into debates trying to convince people that you are right. It's not worth the price of your peace.

Practice remaining calm under pressure so that you don't have to leave the state of relaxation when you feel triggered. As a way to protect your peace, you'll begin to stop attaching your sense of worth to other people's opinion of you.

Affirmations – Spiritual Independence:

"I am enough as I am, right now, in this moment."

"I accept myself deeply and I am proud of myself."

"I release the need to prove myself. I vulnerably relax into being as I am."

"I adore and celebrate the beauty of my unique feminine form."

"I feel secure in who I am. My inner light guides me."

"I forgive myself and others. I lead with empathy."

"I let go of fear. I am held in Divine love."

"I honour my boundaries. I feel secure in myself."

FEELINGS OF THE FEMININE

It would be impossible to talk about embracing a soft life without embodying the right emotional state. Relating to your emotions is essential to embracing an empowered feminine state. And there are a few things you can do to invite softness in your heart:

- *Accept negative feelings*

- *Be authentic with bravery*

- *Indulge in positive feelings*

Accept Negative Feelings

Emotions are a beautiful gift from the Divine. There is no such thing as a 'bad' emotion. They are like the radar signals that help us to navigate through life. In the previous instalment of the femininity series, we discussed how emotions are used as one of the channels to connect with your intuition.

Even though positive emotions are important, the expression of negative emotions is just as essential. Allow these emotions to flow with the same acceptance that you'd give the 'positive' emotions.

So accept that *all* emotions are your friends, even if they feel negative at the time. For example, depression is your body's way of telling you something is wrong. It's your body showing you that it wants the best for you and that it's desperately asking you to make a change.

When negative emotions come up for you, accept them. Don't judge them. Simply see them for what they are. They are showing you where to redirect your awareness. Don't allow emotional triggers to pull you into unsafety, lack of security and hardness. Instead, use it as an opportunity to give these emotions your attention.

At other times, you may feel rage and anger. Don't suppress these emotions. Allow them to be channelled in a manner that's healthy. That's much better than trying to suppress these emotions and denying the opportunity for them to be felt.

It's important to become comfortable watching and detaching yourself from the emotion, understanding that it's simply passing through and you don't have to identify with it. You can express it without being ruled by it.

When you are the patient observer, you get to stay soft because you know that negative feelings do not automatically mean you are unsafe. Negative 'feelings' come and go. So there is no need to run from them, nor should you extend their hold on you.

Acceptance is the route to detached expression. You want to be fully engaged with the emotions you feel, yet you don't want to attach yourself and your sense of identity to them. When an emotion comes through, it's not exactly you. It's just a temporary experience you're having. You don't need to identify with it.

With the example of feeling sad, many people attach themselves to the temporary state of sadness by referring to themselves as a "depressed person", almost as if it's a character trait. They forget that it's simply an emotional state that is present at a specific time and it will go away with the right actions.

With this in mind, don't identify with the negative feelings you experience. Emotions are just passengers on the train and they'll be getting off at some point. If you make these passengers permanent, it will eventually influence the entire journey.

Being in touch with both 'negative' and 'positive' emotions is necessary. The only emotional connections you can heal are those you allow to be felt. Shutting down your connection to them simply results in repression. And it will come out in an unhealthy way one day anyway.

Mentally let yourself know that the bad experiences you've had do not define the potential of what the world wants to give to you. This helps you to feel softer because now you'll be able to remain relaxed amidst the turbulence.

The Power of Expression

Authentic expression is also a significant part of a soft life. When you are in-tune with your authentic expression, your communication becomes stronger, your confidence increases, and you set boundaries.

You gain an increasing capability to attract the right relationships that are perfectly suited to your desires. When you try to fit in and downgrade yourself to match others (or 'fix' your expression to appease others), you will never be secure.

We live in a state of confusion because we are always trying to play a role so that we can fit in with others. Then we complain when our reality doesn't match our personal needs and desires. Why would it? There's no way you can cultivate a reality that is aligned with your true desires when you don't allow yourself to be guided by authenticity.

If you want to tap into this power, take time out to really get to know yourself. Get to know what you like, dislike, hate and love. Be truly vulnerable with yourself and accept whatever answers you are given.

Work on the relationship between you and your feelings, never judging or 'overthinking' them. Listen and accept that how you feel is how *you* feel.

As a feminine woman, you are deeply in-tune with your body, forever checking in and listening to the emotions and sensations that your body evokes. This is your superpower.

And the more you connect with it, the happier you'll be.

One thing to keep in mind is that vulnerable expression is more likely to make an appearance when it's accompanied by security.

Due to our personal fears about what can happen if we embrace this level of authenticity, we will often harden ourselves up in an attempt to protect ourselves from the harshness of the world. But this is why the ability to be vulnerable is a strength.

Not many people are able to open their hearts and embrace the freedom that comes with the feminine spirit.

Not many people can express themselves authentically, nor can they be one with their emotions as they come up. They fear being negatively judged for who they truly are.

When you open up to someone, you are emotionally naked. You are letting them see you behind the mask you put on. There's no more holding onto what you think you should be doing or who you think you should be. You are just 'being'. You are proud to be you and you are giving the world the honour of knowing you. This is the experience that feminine embodiment provides.

So many people will never let the world truly see them. It's understandable when you consider how harsh the world can be. But the confidence that comes from being yourself makes it worth it.

As you practise being authentic, you naturally find that the world is not as scary as you initially thought. You soon find out that people's judgements hold no power, unless *you* give them power.

Affirmations - Acceptance:

"I honour the cycles of life. I flow with what is."

"I honour the flow of my emotions. I embrace my full range of emotions."

"I accept my feelings."

"I connect deeply with myself, with others, and with all of life."

"I trust my inner wisdom. My instincts guide me."

"I forgive the past and live in the present moment."

"I allow myself to be vulnerable and open."

"I am brave enough to be fiercely authentic. My light shines bright unapologetically."

"I'm not afraid to let the world know who I am. I'm proud of myself."

Positive Emotions

One of the best qualities of feminine energy is sensitivity. This might be viewed in a negative way by some people. But wise people see how powerful it can be.

The stimulation that sensitivity provides is what allows you to feel the intensity of a feeling. And fortunately, this remains true when 'positive' emotions are felt.

Indulging in the expression of positive emotions is where femininity truly becomes fun.

A queen in touch with softness wants to live a life of positivity, free from the constraints of misery and struggle. She prioritises feeling good. She likes to giggle. She loves to let loose.

Most people have to go out on a weekend night to feel good. And there's nothing wrong with this. You should absolutely do this too, if that's what gets you going.

However, the problem is when this is the *only* time that you feel good. Every moment of each day contains the potential for this too.

The key is to begin to have a love for yourself that's so intense that you invite positive feelings into as many moments as you can.

Invite love into your reality in every way that you can. You must literally think of yourself as the living expression of love.

Your true essence is the spirit of love. Every fibre of your being, every cell in your body, every thought in your mind should carry the frequency of love.

Ask yourself: *how would I move through life if I were the human embodiment of love?* Love yourself, love others, love the world. Love what you understand, love what you don't understand.

Know that love is flowing through your veins and it's seeping out of your pores. You are breathing it in, just like you do with the air. You need to know that there is an abundant supply of it in your heart and it's never not a part of your being.

Setting boundaries becomes a lot less difficult to enforce when you have love for yourself. Calming yourself down after a stressful situation becomes much easier when you have love. Forgiveness becomes a lot easier when you have love in your heart too.

Fall in love with the idea of love. With your connection to love strengthened, you can now feel an abundance of positivity that ensures that softness is an easy expectation rather than a distant desire.

Affirmations - Self-love:

"I love myself. I love myself. I love myself."

"I'm in love with myself. All of me deserves all of my love."

"I am love. I'm a living embodiment of love."

"I am loved and I am appreciated."

"I am valuable. I am valued."

"I lovingly tend to my inner child with compassion, empathy and attentiveness."

"My feminine power awakens healing, joy and justice in the world."

"I will forever love myself."

"I abundantly trust myself."

"I lovingly care for my needs."

"My heart is my compass."

THE ART OF RECEIVING

One of the most empowering lessons of femininity comes from learning how to receive. Despite this being one of the things that invites paradise into your reality, it's also one of the hardest things for many women to do.

As we touched on in the first book of the Femininity series: *"Healing the Feminine Energy"*, receiving includes being open to the value that the world wants to share with you. This could include receiving assistance, compliments or advice from others. In that book, it covered one of the most important reasons why you should feel okay to receive: because you are worth it.

There are many reasons why women may struggle to receive. But ultimately, it can be put down to fear of something or a lack of self-worth. Once issues surrounding fear are addressed, it becomes much easier to receive all the pleasures that life has to offer.

Many times, the belief that it can be unsafe to receive is a valid one. It's important that we address this so that you are not being blocked from the blessings of life. Giving and receiving is the cycle of the universe. And it's totally okay to be on the receiving end.

Understand that the beliefs you hold will manifest the reality you live in. In the same way that you mustn't identify with certain feelings, you must refrain from attaching yourself to negative experiences that have occurred long ago.

In the past, it may have been the case that you received something that came with a 'catch'. It could have been that you accepted a gift from someone who was just trying to get something from you.

In other cases, you may have allowed a date to treat you to a nice meal, only to find out that they felt that you were obligated to be intimate with them just because they paid for it.

But the first thing to keep in mind is that you are never indebted to anyone for what *they* choose to offer. When a person gives, it should be done for the pleasure of giving, and nothing else.

Of course, the energy of reciprocation is important. However, that must take it's natural course. Otherwise, it's no longer reciprocal. It would be considered transactional.

Regardless of past experiences, a mindset shift is necessary. If you have a mental outlook that affirms that you aren't safe; that men are dangerous; that other women can't be trusted; and that people are out to get you; then this is what becomes your reality and it *will* manifest.

How can you feel confident and empowered if your mind is focused on these kind of things? So watch what you tell your mind. Your mind doesn't care about the nature of what you put into it; it simply works with what you *do* put into it.

If you reaffirm that your environment is safe, that the people around you are trustworthy and that the universe is sending rewards your way, you'll start to walk, talk and move with this frequency.

These beliefs will set a standard that makes sure that it becomes true. You'll remove people (or remove yourself from places) that don't align with your standards. You will selectively focus on being receptive to the things that make you feel safe, soft and serene.

Affirmations: Invite Yourself to Receive:

"I deserve everything the world has to offer."

"It's safe for me to receive."

"I open up to receive support, comfort, and affection."

"I offer space for others to provide value for me."

"I am a beautiful expression of the feminine energy."

"I enjoy receiving and I do so with love, gratitude and appreciation."

"I am worthy of luxury. I deserve the finer things in life."

"I am a magnet for positivity and abundance."

"I am living a serene dream that matches my desires."

Sensuality: Engaging the Body

Receiving from others is important. But allow yourself to take it a step further by tapping into sensuality. This is the route to living an experience where you are receiving on an even deeper level. Femininity is heavily based on 'being' in your body, while being in your head is an attribute of the Masculine.

To "live in your body" means to place your awareness and focus within your movements and actions. The reason why this is powerful is because your sensual side serves as the guide that helps to create a fulfilling life.

As your connection to femininity increases, your desire to receive will increase too. Our bodies are designed for receptivity. Every sense we have is our body's ability to receive from the outer world we're in. Sight, touch, taste and smell are all pathways that allow us to be receptive.

Sensuality is the practice of being in your senses. It allows you to engage with the physical plane as your body interacts with the environment. The goal is to feel deeply present in each action that you carry out, so much so that you enter a state of flow, rather than a state of rigidity.

With this approach, everyday becomes a stimulating experience. Think of your body as a gift that allows you to experience the beauty of life through the senses that you have access to.

Most of us don't truly engage with our senses. Our lives begin to feel so repetitive that we simply do things for the sake of it. But this is what makes life feel monotonous.

Sex is the first thing that comes to mind for many people when sensuality is mentioned. But sensuality doesn't automatically refer to the experience of sex. The two can be linked. But that is just one part of the experience.

Sensuality can be so much more than just bedroom intimacy. It can be a way of living.

Think back to any time that you've seen women who ooze this type of vibe. You can feel their feminine presence. They are connected to their feminine energy, so they live life fully engaged with their emotions and their environment.

They have anchored themselves in softness and comfort. They allow their bodies to serve as the compass that shows the route to pleasure and peace.

With a sensual approach to life, you are prioritising an experience that pleases your senses. Feminine women love to live in the present because it's in the current moment where all of the pleasure exists.

One of the best ways to embody this level of presence is by getting into the habit of slowing down. This does a lot to quiet any chaos within.

Add an aura of peace to your actions by being slow and intentional. Many times, we rush our movements, which induces a sense of panic. We think with urgency that makes our mind chaotic.

Slowing down reverses the process and invites calmness to replace all anxiety. Life can feel fast-paced but it doesn't mean you have to match it.

You have to stop and think: is there a need to rush? What's the worst thing that will happen if I slow things down right now? How important is the task I am doing, and is it worth stressing over?

You'll often find that you stress over things that aren't worth it. Prioritise your emotional comfort over the completion of a task that doesn't hold true meaning.

Intentionality is the icing on top to add with slowness. Being intentional with your movements is great for activating presence.

Whatever you do, do it with assurance and belief. If you do things half-heartedly, half of your attention will be in your head. This takes you out of your body.

In the next section of this chapter, we will go over ways that you can live a life that pleases your senses and increases feminine energy.

Affirmations - Bodily Appreciation:

"My body is my home."

"No matter where I am or what is going on, I am at home in my body."

"It's a gift to be embodied as a woman."

"There is so much security within my body."

"It feels so safe to be in my body."

"I am so grateful for my body."

"I adore every inch of me."

"My body looks great. My body feels amazing."

"Being in my body feels natural to me."

"I'm here to listen to the wisdom of my body and receive all that it wants me to know."

"I lovingly care for my body and I nourish my soul."

"My outer beauty is a reflection of my inner radiance."

The Senses of the Body: Eyes

An important part of sensual embodiment includes being conscious about what you receive through the sense of sight. We experience things, faces and places by using our eyes. We are looked at and we look at the world around us.

The best way we can show gratitude for eyesight is by fully indulging in the gift that the Divine has given us. The first thing that you should seek to admire through your eyes is your reflection in the mirror. It's much easier to feel soft-hearted when you feel like you are an expression of beauty. The sight of yourself should fill you with love and gratitude.

Insecurities are a normal part of life. We all have them. For most of us, there will be things that we wish we could change or improve. But that should never stop us from loving ourselves.

You cannot look like anyone else, nor can you be anyone else. So don't get into a habit of comparison when it comes to the looks or expression of another person. Simply admire them for their qualities, but admire yourself for your qualities too.

This is easier said than done for many of us. It can be hard to look and simply admire our physique. However, you have the power to ensure that your mind is not filled with negative self-talk.

The Senses of the Body: Sound

The more that your world is an affirmation of softness, the more soft you will feel. So it's important to listen to sound frequencies that echo this sentiment.

If you like to listen to music, choose the type that makes you feel sensual. Make it a fun adventure to explore the options that are available.

Music can have a profound effect on your state of mind. Studies suggest that the frequency of the music (measured in Hertz) influences how you feel. Some songs induce anxiety, whilst others can make you feel calm. There is music that makes you tired, but there is also music that helps to heal you.

Turn on music that makes you want to physically flow and move in a way that releases all anxiety. Motion helps to release tension.

As we discussed in the previous volume of the book series, movement is very important to the Feminine and music helps with that.

Note that sensual music doesn't automatically mean 'sexual' music. In fact, much of the music today that is very sexual is not sensual at all. We are living in an era where sensual music is not as heavily promoted.

Much of the music today interacts with our body in a negative way. So be conscious of the music that you listen to and seek the sound frequencies that soothe, heal and bring out your sensual side.

The Senses of the Body: Smell

We don't actively use our noses as frequently as our eyes. But it still counts as one of the most potent ways to connect to sensuality. When it comes to scents, you should be taking advantage of the opportunity to enrich your nose with beautiful smells.

This could include you taking in the scents of the meals that you are cooking but it also extends to smelling the food that others have made for you.

The next time you are eating at a nice restaurant, enjoy the scent of the food or drink before you taste it.

This is how you transform the experience of eating from being a boring meal to an exquisite evening out that connects you to feminine presence.

Great activities to do include going out shopping for things that give off beautiful scents. This could be taking in the scents of flowers when you go plant shopping.

Going even further though, smelling great for yourself is also important. So consider investing in a new perfume or two.

Getting the right perfume doesn't happen instantly. What most people do is they just buy popular perfumes, many times without even trying it themselves.

You should be looking for perfumes that match your character and this can take some time to find. So it usually requires going out to sample and test different perfumes.

Get scents that make *you* feel feminine. Do it for you and nobody else. So even when you aren't around anyone, you can still wear it.

You don't have to do this all of the time but wearing it for yourself still makes you feel good. And that's all it's about.

The Senses of the Body: Taste

One of our favourite activities to do as humans is to eat. It makes perfect sense considering the fact that we need it to survive. However, only living life with "survival" in mind is not a feminine approach to life.

The Feminine embraces pleasure. And an abundance of pleasure is at the tip of the tongue when you make time for good dining experiences.

It's nice to make food for yourself at home but it can be a much better experience to go out for some fine dining once in a while. It's not just about the food. It's about the ritualistic opportunity to connect to your senses.

One of the best things about fine dining is that the atmospheres in these establishments are usually designed to be sensually pleasing.

From the architectural decor of the walls to the sound of the music, or from the level of lighting to the presentation of the food on the plate, everything is designed to give you an experience that feels pleasurable. And of course, the food itself is usually tasty. Intentionally take in the entire experience in a way that enlivens all of your senses.

The Senses of the Body: Touch

One of the other senses we use just as often as sight is the sense of touch. Could you imagine a world without the ability to physically feel things? It would be as if we were ghosts lacking the ability to connect to our reality. It's something we take for granted. But it's one of the ways you can truly stimulate your senses.

Feeling the touch of your own body is definitely important. So do things that nourish and heal your skin.

Go down the rabbit-hole of research and see what you can do to improve the state of your body. It could include nurturing your skin with high-quality products that are healthy and designed to leave you feeling great.

Try facial treatments and mud baths/masks. All of this enhances the vibrancy, brightness and hydration of your face.

See all of this as an investment in your health. Don't look at these things as a chore. It's not something you *have* to do. It's something you *get* to do.

Changing your perspective strongly changes how you feel. Think of these things like a ceremony of rejuvenation. Make it a ritualistic activity, whether it be a night-time face-routine or an evening shave.

See it as a celebration of your body and an act of ultimate self-care. View it as an opportunity to connect to your body and pour positive affirmations into it while you nurture it.

As you shave and run the razor down your leg, observe how beautiful your skin looks and feel it's smoothness afterwards.

Also, make time to have baths that feel ritualistic and relaxing. Treat it like a time to celebrate your feminine essence.

Put on soft music that evokes a blissful feeling and light up aromatic candles for beautiful scents. When you step into the bath, feel the warmth of the water as it flows against your body.

After cleansing your skin, run your fingers across your body in a sensual manner and feel them glide over your skin. Do it slowly and in an intentionally sensual manner. Admire every inch of yourself as you do it. Let the ceremony run for as long as you desire.

The ceremony doesn't need to stop there though. When applying lotion, do it with the aura of sensuality to prolong your ritual.

As you cream each body part, speak words of gratitude. Continue feeling and believing that this is not just a regular wash, but that it's the cleansing ceremony of a Queen.

Affirmations - Sensual Connection:

"My sensuality is sacred, healing, and an expression of self-love."

"I don't apologise for wanting to live a pleasurable life with pleasurable experiences."

"I celebrate my body's unique capacity for sensual pleasure."

"My pleasure is a top priority in my life and I give myself permission to pursue what brings me delight."

"I embrace the feeling of passion. I welcome erotic energy into my life."

"I am grateful for my sexuality and sensual body."

"I welcome intimacy into my relationships."

"I release any guilt or shame around my natural sensuality."

"I embrace touching, adorning and caring for my sensual form."

FEMININE EXPRESSION

Be the Expression of Beauty

The impressive presence of feminine energy is instantly recognisable when an empowered woman walks into the room. The power is shared through her aura, her skin and how she carries herself.

A woman who moves with sensuality provides an intoxicating experience to the people around her. People want to be around her because it feels like a vacation away from life's troubles. She has this effect because the feeling of paradise lives within her.

The soft life of a feminine woman starts from within. However, the vibe you project to the world is just as important. It's important to be aware of how you express yourself.

Communication and presentation are the tools that tell the world who you are. With this in mind, what are your outward expressions and interactions broadcasting to others about who you are?

The energy you embody tells the world how to interact with you. When you move through the world with confidence, relaxation and magnetism, the world has to interact with you based on that frequency.

Depending on where you are in life, this can be difficult. Adopting a feminine tone of expression may feel out of the ordinary compared to what you are used to.

You may have hardened up to match the toughness of the world so it became natural to express yourself in a masculine manner. But this is an invitation for you to upgrade how you express yourself.

Adopt feminine mannerisms instead. This relates to the presentation of your outer appearance (such as hands, face, clothes and shoes). However, it can and does go much deeper than that.

The Feminine Voice

As discussed in the previous book of the series, beautifying how you look, as well as the aesthetics of your environment certainly helps to increase feminine energy.

The way you relate to the expression of beauty will have a profound effect on how you feel. So it's great to make an effort in this area.

However, it's just as important to project feminine beauty through your verbal communication too. The way you speak represents the energy that you have.

Have you ever talked with someone who spoke nice words on the surface but their voice tone told another story? Feminine and masculine expressions work in the same way.

There are many women who look soft and feminine but when they speak they come across as masculine.

There is nothing wrong with this if this is what you want. But if you're trying to create a world of softness for yourself, this way of communicating will not help to birth that reality.

Nowadays many women are encouraged to speak with more vulgarity and loudness. At times, it may even be necessary.

In specific situations, such as at work or in conflict, it can make sense to communicate in this manner. However, this doesn't stimulate feminine energy and it's best not to make it a habit. Don't forget that softness can be just as potent in getting you what you want.

Work on your awareness of the feeling that your voice tone is likely to incite in others. Pay attention to how you're coming across to other people. It is good to ask yourself the question: *what vibe is my communication projecting?*

Start with becoming aware of your voice tone. It represents the flavour of your spirit. A loud or harsh tone communicates hardness. A voice with flow and softness comes across as feminine.

Everyone is able to adjust how they communicate. We do it naturally all of the time. How you speak with your partner on a romantic night is very different to how you speak at work when you're leading a team meeting. Consciously adjust your verbal communication and tone to the situation you are in.

The following points are different aspects of your verbal communication that you should be aware of and how different situations can influence it:

- **Voice resonance:** What situations encourage your voice to be light and gentle compared to when it's deep and aggressive?

- **Speed:** When do you notice yourself trying to blurt words out with quickness compared to when you are comfortable speaking in a relaxed manner?

- **Temperature:** What situations bring out a cold, monotonous tone and when do you notice your voice being warm, lively and friendly?

- **Word choice:** Be conscious of the effect that certain words have on people and how it influences the direction of the conversation.

As you gain more awareness of your communication, you'll see how much influence you have over people in your interactions. You'll realise how much you can control the vibe of the conversation when you are the one setting the tone.

For example, when you feel like you are in a disagreement with someone, you could expect that the conversation can become combative if you start speaking quicker, with a deep tone and harsh words. In the end, you are the one that also suffers because if the conversation turns ugly, then it no longer feels safe.

However, if you remain controlled in the disagreement, then there is a higher chance that the conversation remains calm. Most people react to the tone that the other person sets. You must make the intention to be the one that sets the tone.

Also, take note of the people that bring out the hard side of your communication. It could be a new potential partner that you're getting to know. Do you notice whether they bring out a soft, relaxed style of communication, or is it the opposite? When you are stressed, your tone will naturally become deeper, harder and more masculine.

Your verbal communication style is able to warn you when you don't feel safe around someone. So if you notice tension in your expression, it's an indication that you don't feel safe around this person. This is the time to decide whether you want to allow them to remain in your presence.

Another important part of feminine communication is classiness. In a society that supports degeneracy and tastelessness, it's a breath of fresh air to be the type of person who doesn't feel the need to continuously speak immodestly.

Refrain from being quick to cuss and be conscious of offending others with your words. This doesn't mean that you should be a people pleaser. But it does mean that you should be mindful of other people's feelings when you speak to them.

This also means that you should be mindful of the environment that you are in. Refrain from speaking loudly where it's not necessary. Speaking in a calm tone can be effective in getting your point across. You don't have to rely on masculine communication, unless the situation truly calls for it (such as when you feel unsafe).

All of this is easy to do when there is no pressure in a situation. However, when you are in high-pressure situations, that's when you'll get to see how much control you have over your communication style.

When other people would typically resort to chaotic communication is when all of the work really counts. Will you allow the circumstance to pull you out of a feminine state?

If possible, it's much better to establish firm boundaries and remove yourself from places that threaten the expression of your feminine energy. You are the one who benefits from this more than anyone else because it will feel much better to be where it feels safe.

Empowered Body Language

Another crucial element of feminine communication is being aware of your body language. What is your body conveying that your words aren't? Body language speaks way more than your words alone ever will. Your body carries the essence of your feminine spirit.

We all already know this on some level. Imagine if someone gave you a compliment, but they also had an extremely negative expression on their face. It's likely that you would've instantly felt and knew that their words didn't align with their energy.

It's clear that we are more likely to trust non-verbal communication over the words that people use. In the previous example, you would assume that how they truly feel is different from what they're saying even if the words are really nice on the surface.

On the deepest level, communication is the transmission of information that represents what we are truly thinking and what our spirit is feeling. It doesn't matter what you say if the energy doesn't match it.

Body language can differ depending on the personal character and cultural expression of a person. However, the fundamentals of feminine communication remain the same. It's important to communicate warmth and elegance through eye contact, smiling and body positioning.

Expressing yourself in an empowered way also requires self-confidence. Your movements should be laced with the belief that you know you are a walking expression of beauty and value. Every action should carry conviction and this level of belief is what births charisma.

It's also important to be conscious of when your body language projects a sense of hardness. Aside from when you feel unsafe, it is generally beneficial to present yourself in a way that is open and inviting. Looking away when in conversation, crossing arms, huffing and puffing are all ways to create a disconnect whilst you're talking with someone.

Remember, that in the same way that self-affirmations are important in reaffirming the vibe that you want to embody, the way you present yourself to others is also influential. When you engage with people, you reaffirm to them who you are and what aura you have.

The perception that others have of you will heavily affect how they treat you, which then affects your emotional state. It's an energetic cycle that can help to support the type of person you want to be.

If you communicate in a confident way, then people simply assume that you are a person worth respecting. If you lack belief in your presentation, it can be felt. This will then communicate to the person that you aren't a special individual worth treating in special ways.

So it's essential that you carry an abundance of self-love and confidence. Know that you are favoured by the Divine, so that your spirit commands your reality to serve you and submit to your standards.

Affirmations - Soft Expression:

"I am the living expression of softness."

"I rest in the strength of my feminine power."

"My warmth and presence is felt by everyone around me."

"I am forever exuding feminine aura.

"I walk with grace. My actions are graceful."

"I soften my voice and my touch."

"I communicate with elegance."

"My voice conveys warmth."

"My actions carry the frequency of femininity."

CONCLUSION

Embrace a Soft Life

Unfortunately, our society is not currently one that supports the expression of feminine energy. Many women are being encouraged to abandon the power of their femininity. They are being taught that the only way to express strength is through the expression of masculinity.

Since the system won't take on the responsibility to create a world where the expression of divine feminine qualities are nurtured, *we* have to be the change that we want to see.

It's important to remember that your external environment reflects your internal one. This is empowering because it guarantees that you are the one that's in the driver's seat. You are in complete control of your spiritual destiny.

You can influence your environment so that it becomes a reflection of your softness. It's a journey that never ends. But it's certainly one that will pay off forever.

You must take pride in your femininity and you must let go of the thoughts, things and people who don't support you living in the highest level of satisfaction. Take control of your mind, nurture your spirit and tend to your needs.

Don't fall into the trap of allowing negative thoughts to persist, as many other people do. Make a real commitment to create the conditions that give you access to a feeling of peace.

Most people chase happiness, but they fail in this task because they're always looking outside of themselves. Know that all of the answers lay within.

Doing this will affect all external things that impact you. You'll begin to choose high-quality partners that support your vision and you will align with sisters who help to heal your heart. Even things like your career will be influenced by your desire to create sources of income that nurture a softer state of being.

Remember, a woman's greatest strength is her femininity. So don't let the world ever tell you any different. Feminine energy is like the compass that will guide you to a level of fulfilment that many people dream of.

Make sure you trust that guidance and have no doubt about the destination it will lead you to. You've got this.

ENDING PAGE

There will be those who ask things like "what if I
don't meet a man who supports my softness?" or
"how can I be feminine and still get things done?!".
These are the type of things that will be addressed
in other volumes of the Femininity series, because
there is so much to unpack.

It's definitely true that it's much easier to remain in
a feminine frame when you have healthy
masculinity around. It's also the case that you will
need to express masculine energy at times to
protect your softness. There will be scenarios that
require you to be the loud and tenacious version of
yourself rather than the soft and relaxed version.

It would be unrealistic to assume that most women
can be fully in their feminine energy all of the time.
But the motivation behind this book is to remind you
that softness is a state that is easier to attain than
you think.

Reading all of this information is not worth it if you
don't make it a part of your life. Seek to be the
embodiment of the knowledge so that it genuinely

influences your daily experiences. These books are designed to be bite-sized so that you can properly digest the tips before moving on to the next part of the series.

As you read each volume of the series and you continue to develop your connection to feminine energy, all of the questions you have will be answered.

This is not a quick-fix. It's a journey that takes time. However, as the journey unfolds, everything that you need to access your highest level of fulfilment will be revealed. Know that I have no doubt that you'll get to the destination that you need to get to.

If there is anything that you would like to be addressed in future resources, please feel free to email me at: ReemusBailey@GMAIL.com. You can also comment/message on one of my social media accounts: @ReemusB (TikTok & Instagram).

Check out my website ReemusB.com for information on how you can book sessions if you would like to work with me to balance your masculine-feminine energies.

Made in the USA
Las Vegas, NV
29 December 2023